Where are the walks?

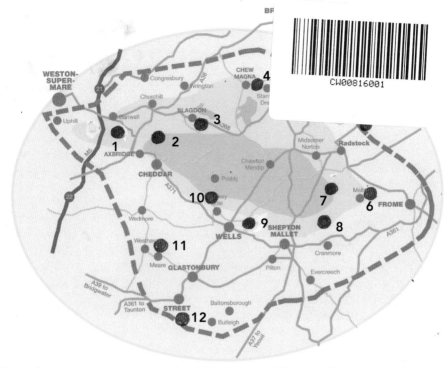

The yellow border marks the circulation area of Mendip Times magazine

The peak of perfection

From Kings Wood car park, near Winscombe. 6.1 miles, or 6.4 miles (to Cross and pub). 3-3.5 hours walking.
OS Explorer Map 153 Weston-super-Mare, ref 420 559

Refreshment: Pubs in Cross

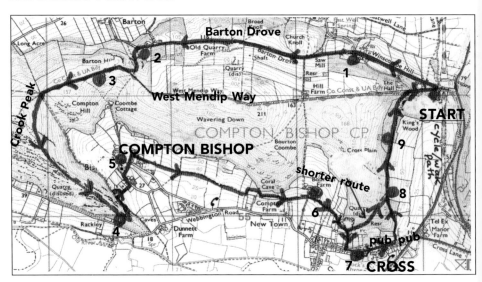

THIS invigorating circle aims to provide a more unusual, gentler and more varied route than normal for enjoying the exhilarating heights and views of Crook Peak, one of the most dramatic hills on the West Mendip plateau.

The exploration follows an old drove under the northern edge and then climbs quite quickly to the Wavering Down ridge. It's up to you if you wish to go up the Peak or not! The route then travels round the curving ridge before dropping to Compton Bishop from where a pretty path leads through fields along the southern edge with an option of visiting a pub in Cross. The walk's end provides a good contrast, through ancient Kings Wood.

TERRAIN: Walking on lanes, tracks and field footpaths, mainly dry underfoot. There is a steep but short climb up onto Wavering Down, a climb if you go up the Peak, and another very short uphill stretch after the pub. Otherwise the route is gently undulating. There are several stiles.

PARK in the National Trust car park for Kings Wood, just off the A38, between Winscombe and Cross. If coming from the north, pass the garage and then turn right on Winscombe Hill. The car park is shortly on the left.

START: Turn left along the lane, which is not busy and gives good views over the valley and across to Wales on a clear day. After about nine minutes pass a road bends sign, and shortly past this, turn up left on a drive/track

1. BARTON DROVE
This is Barton Drove, an ancient thoroughfare across Mendip for moving animals. We follow it for about 1.5 miles. It rises gently and then levels out. It is an attractive path below the hill with good views. Eventually cross a stile into a meadow. Follow the left edge and then go left over a stile and continue on in the same direction with the fence on your right. Cross a stile in the corner and carry on. Join a path and follow it to a stile at the end.

2. CLIMB
You are in an Open Access area and the climb begins: turn left up the track and as it enters trees, fork up right and follow the path up onto the open land. Cross a stile ahead by a gate and come onto the West Mendip Way and Wavering Down. Your reward on a clear day should be some tremendous views over Somerset and to Crook Peak for the next stretch.

3. WEST MENDIP WAY
Turn right. You may well see some of the distinctive White Park cattle introduced to control vegetation. Follow the wall and then descend to a marker post. To ascend Crook Peak itself go straight on up and then turn left down to rejoin the main route. So for the main route, fork left and go along under the left side of the peak (don't drop down).
Continue along a grassy ridge, so you have made a horseshoe shape from where you came onto Wavering Down. There are fine views over the Levels and over Compton Bishop village and the Down behind. Go on as far as you can, dropping down.

4. BARRIER
Go through a wooden barrier and turn left down a path under trees. Go on through a gate and on down to a T-junction in Compton Bishop.

5. COMPTON BISHOP
Turn left passing the old Manor House and come to the church.

St Andrew's was consecrated in 1236. Inside the church is a fine pulpit, the remains of c14th glass and an interesting double piscina.

Turn right on Church Lane and at a junction, go straight ahead along the marked footpath track. It bends round right, servicing one or two houses and then goes into a stable yard. Keep straight on over a stile and on through several fields following the right hedge. Up on your left towers Wavering Down.
Reach a garden fence and house ahead. Follow the fence left around the garden. Cross a stile and maintain your earlier direction. Go down the length of the field, over a stile and then bend right in the next field following the right hedge. Cross a stile and continue with telegraph poles on your left. Come down on to a farm drive.

6. FARM DRIVE
Cross and go on to cross a stile ahead. Follow the right hedge and go over another stile and along the hedge. Go through a kissing gate and on with hedge still on the right. Then as the hedge bends, head across

the field bearing right to the far side where you find a ladder stile left over a wall. Go through a disused quarry staying on the right.

Options: To stay on the hill and not visit Cross: (this route is easier, a little shorter and prettier): Ignore the stile right and continue on and then bend left with the wall on your right and climb a little. These rocky slopes are an ideal wild flower habitat. As you progress, get good views across the Levels and along the Mendip ridge. Continue to follow the path until you reach a crossing of paths. Turn left and follow from - 8 Crossing Path.

Options: For the pub and Cross village, still in the quarry area, turn right over a marked stile and follow the path down, over a stile and through a gate to the road in Cross.

7. CROSS
Turn left and after a few minutes reach an old coaching inn, the White Hart. (serves lunch 12-2pm). If you want a pub open all day, go on a few more yards to the New Inn.
It's another half hour back to the start. To continue the round, shortly

past the White Hart, just before the 30 mile sign, turn up left on a steep small path (unmarked). It's steep, narrow and rocky for a short section and then becomes easier. Go through a wooden gate into the Crook Peak area. Continue along the bridleway near the right edge. After about a minute reach a crossing path. Here the non pub walkers join. Go straight over.

8. CROSSING PATH
After another couple of minutes enter woodland – the ancient Kings Wood. At a fork in the path, go either way – it all meets up. Continue on.

9. LARGE GATE
Go through a large wooden gate. Reach a marker post and a clearing (still under trees) whichis a path junction. Here, <u>continue on</u> but take the left hand path (the higher path). Go through a wooden hunting gate and continue on to a wide crossing track. Turn right. Follow this down through the wood to the car park.

The White Hart, Cross, 01934 732260
The New Inn, Cross, 01934 732455

4

To the hillfort

From Shipham. About 6 miles, 3 hours walking.
OS Explorer Map 155, Bristol and Bath, ref: 577 630

Refreshment: pubs at Churchill and Star and a pub and coffee shop in Shipham

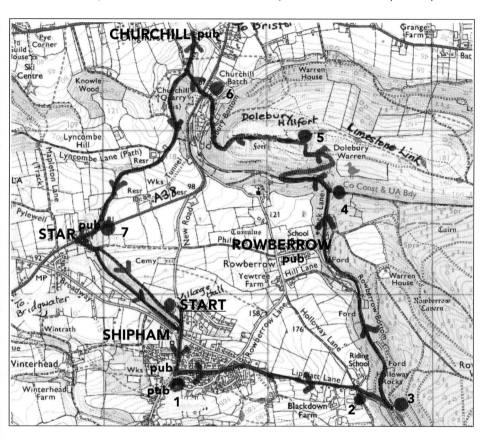

THIS is a 'star' walk in more ways than one. Starting from Shipham in the Area of Outstanding Natural Beauty, it combines woodland walking with open top high land up on Dolebury Hill Fort. There are two really good pubs en route to make the going easier and one of these is in the hamlet of Star.

TERRAIN: The route takes in one very

steep, stepped climb onto the hillfort and some paths may be rather uneven and rocky under foot, so wear good boots or shoes. As usual, expect some mud after rain.   It is a great walk for observing wildflowers and butterflies. Bring the dog, too.

PARK: Shipham village, one of the few villages on the Mendip plateau, about 0.75 miles off the A38 Bristol-

Exeter road, south of the traffic lights at Churchill, Turn off by the garage. Park in the spacious village hall car park, on the right as you approach the village from the A38.

START: From the village hall, turn right on the main road to the village.

1. GREEN
At the green (The Square) turn left up the Hollow, past Lenny's Coffee Shop.

This is a friendlly community cafe run in aid of St Leonard's Church.

Fork right on Barnpool. Reach a junction at a grassy triangle and turn right. Follow it all the way, gently climbing past houses. At the top go ahead on the marked path into Rowberrow Warren woods.

2. ROWBERROW WARREN
The stony track drops downhill to reach a junction at the stream by a Bristol Water enclosure.

The crossing path was the route, known as the Slaggers Path, taken by miners from Shipham and Rowberrow in the late c19th when mining for lead and calamine in their areas had ceased and they sought work at the Charterhouse mineries.

3. STREAM
Don't cross the stream. Instead turn left on the bridleway to Rowberrow following the stream on your right. Ignore any side turns. Eventually pass two or three pretty country cottages, as well as a few ruins in the under-growth of former miners cottages. At a white cottage keep straight on along the path to Appletree Cottage.

Pass close to the cottage and go through a metal gate. Pass a stable and come again into woodland. There is a footpath at the side of the main track which can get very muddy.

4. T-JUNCTION
Reach a junction with a main track which runs along underneath Dolebury hillfort and turn left. After three minutes, take a stile on right, some-what hidden in the trees.

This is the National Trust's Dolbury Warren and the steep hillfort bank is ahead. The Warren is a Site of Special Scientific Interest, rich with grassland flowers and at least 30 species of butterflies.

Bear right on a small path through the trees and gradually bear over to the left to the bottom of the hill. The path climbs up, becomes steep and then stepped and bends up onto the open grassy slopes. There's a great view over the wooded valley with the church and old manor of Rowberrow. At the top follow the path a short way and then cross right over a stile. Continue straight up to reach a crossing path. Turn left. Cross a stile and reach Dolebury hillfort.

5. HILLFORT
This Iron Age hillfort is a Scheduled Ancient Monument and Site of Special Scientific Interest.

You are now near the south east corner of the fort and want to make for the 'gate' on the western edge. You can go straight ahead along this path going just below the edge, bend round right at the end and then turn left to leave by the western 'gate'.

But for the best views and to get a feel of the place go more into the heart. So go right up along the bank on a smallpath. At a small crossing path, turn left over the banks and ditch and into the fort.

The fort also did service as a rabbit warren providing food for the local people and ahead you may see the ruins of the keeper's cottage .
On a clear day the views take in the Welsh coast and hills, down the Mendip spine to Brean Down, Steep Holm and Flat Holm, over Wrinton Vale and down to Quantock and Exmoor.

Go straight ahead across and down through the grassy fort and leave by the western 'gate'. The stony path bends left and winds down. Go through a hunting gate and on down. Turn right on the tarmac lane through the hamlet of Dolbury Bottom to the busy A38.

6. MAIN ROAD
Cross with care and follow the stony bridleway on the other side, uphill. Reach a junction at the top with a track - the old Bristol Road. Our circle continues by going left, but for the renowned cottage pub, the Crown Inn, turn right for a few minutes down the track and then return. To continue, follow the track uphill looking across to Lyncombe Hill. Ignore side paths. At a Bristol Water enclosure, keep straight on all the way to Star and the A38.

7. STAR
Turn right to the Star Inn, which has served travellers over the years. Carry on past it, cross the A38 and go up Cheddar Combe. Pass a line of old miners' cottages. Here is a choice of routes back to Shipham.
The first is gentler, but more enclosed, up a stony bridleway through the combe, known as *Daffodil Valley* and in Spring you may hope to see daffodils and bluebells. For this, keep straight on. It comes out onto a side road at the top. Turn left to the main road and left again to the village hall. But for the more open route which I prefer, turn left by the miners' cottages over a stile into the field. Parallel the left fence for about 60 yards and then bear up right onto a bank, passing to the left of a fence, sealing off an old mine entrance. Continue uphill going to the left of a telegraph pole. From here you can see Dolbury fort very clearly. Continue to the village hall.

The Crown, Churchill, 01934 852995
The Star Inn, Star, 01934 842569
The Miner's Arms, Shipham,
01934 842146
The Penscot, Shipham, 01934 842659

To the pub by the stream

From Blagdon. About 5.5 miles, 2.5 hours walking.

OS Explorer Map 141, Cheddar Gorge & Mendip Hills West , ref: 501 591

Refreshment: Pub in Rickford. Ice cream van, Burrington Ham!

Particularly good at bluebell time!

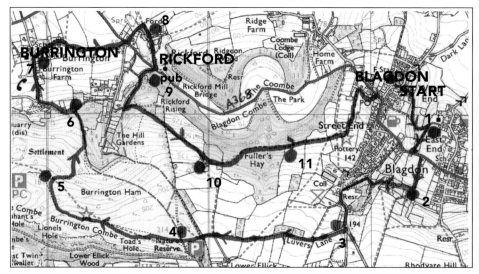

A PERFECT walk on a clear day in the Area of Outstanding Natural Beauty on the northern Mendip escarpment above Blagdon. It goes across Burrington Ham and down to Burrington hamlet and then to picturesque Rickford with its ford. There's the chance of a stop at the stream-side pub in Rickford before rising for even more great views and then through shady bluebell woodland before descending to Blagdon.

TERRAIN: There are two hills but the rest is quite easy walking on dry paths and it is a good dog circle too.

PARK: In the free car park in Blagdon behind Blagdon Village Club down Station Road. Turn in left by the fire station. Blagdon is on the A368 road from Churchill to Bath.

START: Go out the car park by the way you came in and turn left a few yards downhill. Turn right into Bell Square and go through picking up a tarmac path. This connects both sides of Blagdon and gives great views across Blagdon lake and valley and across to the impressive church tower of St Andrew's Blagdon. Follow the path round and down, through a gate and along, through another gate by a natural spring, Tim's Well, once the only source of water for the village, and then turn left and head up towards the church.

1. CHURCH

This beautiful church dates back to 1907/9 when it was built by William Henry Wills on a site where there had been a church since the c14th.

Just before the churchyard gate turn right along the green bank at the top of the small valley. Follow this to the road, looking down right across to the village orchard.

Turn left on the pavement, separated from the road by a grass verge. Soon, turn right across the verge and cross the road. Ascend Slad Acre Lane opposite. After a few minutes, before reaching a house ahead, turn right on the drive.

2. CATTLE GRID

Cross a cattle grid at the start and follow the drive. As the hedges begin, take the marked footpath right until you reach tarmac. Continue on, dropping down to a junction of ways. Turn left on the marked footpath which bizarrely goes through the garage of Glen Cottage, up steps and up the garden. Continue up through a glorious, 'secret' green valley carpeted with garlic, mosses and full of bird song. Go up steps at the top quite steeply and along to Rhodyate Lane. Turn left uphill for a couple of minutes and at the start of Ellick Road, go right on the right of way, known as Luvers Lane.

3. LUVERS LANE

Follow this tarmac path along the top of the hill. Go through a gate ahead into a field and now maintain direction, following the left hedge through three fields until you come out onto Burrington Ham Open Access Area.

To continue the round, carry on round to the right a few yards only and then turn down left on a path, with the end of the rocks over on your left. Reach an open area and continue on, bearing slightly right following a path through bracken along the side of the open area. Continue to the foot of a line of silver birches. Here turn right under the birch avenue. It bends down left, and leads to a T-junction with another path. Turn left and follow this track downhill. It goes through a small open area where the hummocks and bumps remind us of former mining. A gate leads onto the Link, an unmade residential road above Burrington.

4. THE HAM
Head straight across Burrington Ham where recently there has been some investigation into an early medieval settlement there. Ignore side paths and crossing tracks. Follow a yellow footpath arrow on, going out into one of my favourite areas of the Ham with great views on either side – left up across to Black Down, right over Wrington Vale and ahead across the Severn Estuary to Wales.

There has been much clearance opening up the area and allowing better views and wild flowers.

If you wish, after a while you can walk out on the left side of the ridge getting better views across over Burrington Combe to Black Down. But when you get as far as you can the track bends down right (north) and ahead you can see Long Rock.

5. LONG ROCK
Drop down to reach the foot of the rocks and climb up for the best views.

6. THE LINK
Turn left. Drop down to a triangle of grass and a junction. Here turn right downhill, passing the former village pound and coming into Burrington.

7. BURRINGTON
The church is well worth a visit. At the small square, turn right on the No Through lane past pretty cottages and on as it becomes a tarmac path leading to the main road.
Cross and go down opposite into Rickford and its picturesque ford.

8. RICKFORD
Bend right through this peaceful hamlet and reach a traditional English pub, the Plume of Feathers with tables outside overlooking the stream.

It links up to the River Yeo. Rickford has its own natural spring attached to Blagdon's lake. Its clear waters support water crowsfoot, watercress and yellow monkey musk. It is also

the scene of a very popular annual
charity duck race.

Continue on past the Victorian gauge
house from which Bristol Water
controls the stream from the lake. It
gravitates by pipeline into Blagdon
Lake. Reach the main road.

The lake was once a millpond serving a
flourishing flour mill and later a paper
mill. The church, originally a Baptist
chapel, is now a Masonic lodge.

9. MAIN ROAD
This is a blind bend on a busy road so
take care. Cross and turn right.
Almost immediately take the footpath
left which climbs through woodland.
Ignore a side turn and carry on up,
passing a beautiful garden down right,
just before you go through a gate
onto a crossing track. Turn left uphill.
Continue on and cross a cattle grid,
climbing up through an open area with
glorious views over Wrington Vale and
across to Wales. Cross another cattle
grid and come to a farm.

10. FARM
Turn left at the side of a stone barn,
following the footpath. Continue on,
entering woodland. Fork left and go
through an area called Fuller's Hay
which in spring is a carpet of bluebells.
Descend gradually and after several
minutes, the path drops down more
steeply to cross a small valley and
carries on. Eventually reach a field.

11. FIELD
Turn left with woodland on your left.
Cross a stile/barrier into a field and
go straight across. Cross another
barrier by a gate and here get a great
view of Blagdon Lake.
Go straight ahead ignoring a crossing
path and near the far side, turn left
down a spur of the field. Cross a stile
in the corner and maintain direction.
In the bottom corner a kissing gate
leads to a track. Turn right to the
road in Blagdon. Cross to the Village
Club and go through to the car park.

Plume of Feathers, Rickford,
01761 462 682

Past the ancient stones

From Chew Magna. About 6 miles, 3 hours walking
OS Explorer Map 155, Bristol and Bath, ref: 577 630

Refreshment: Pubs in Stanton Drew and at Newtown and pubs and cafe in Chew Magna.

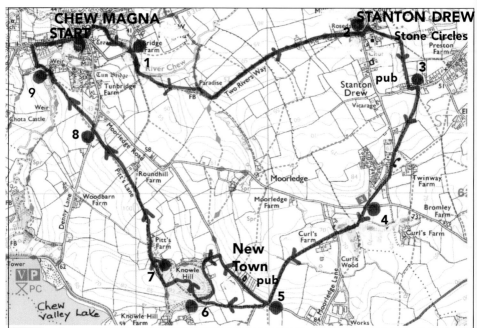

VISIT the ancient standing stones at Stanton Drew on this moderate circle in the beautiful North Somerset countryside around Chew Valley Lake. En route there are glorious views across Chew Valley Lake from Knowle Hill.

TERRAIN: There are two or three gentle hills and one steep, but short ascent. Walking is made easier because of the many metal kissing gates which have replaced traditional stiles. This makes it a comfortable dog walk. Muddy in parts after rain.

PARK: In Chew Magna. Find a space in the village car park behind the Pelican Inn at the east end of the High Street, or failing that, park somewhere else suitable. You could also arrive here by bus.

START: At the entrance to the church at the east end of the High Street. Walk into the churchyard towards the main church door and then half way along, bear right and follow a smaller, tarmac path in the churchyard which hugs a stone wall on the right. Cross a low stone and pipe stile and continue ahead on the drive, bearing round right, past the entrance to historic Chew Court. The beautiful drive takes you out under trees and past mossy staddle stones. Pass the picturesque cricket field right.

1. MAIN ROAD

Cross the main road through the gate opposite and then go ahead in the field to another gate in the far left corner. Cross the bridge over the River Chew and continue along a track with the river on your left. Bend left with the river and continue on a smaller track, climbing gently with the river below. Maintain direction to a field corner. Here, stay in the field and bend round right along the edge. Soon go left over a stile.

Follow a clear path across the field and drop down into a valley by pines. Cross a footbridge and go ahead to a footpath marker pole and a crossing track, the Two Rivers Way. For much of its journey this follows the Chew all the way to the River Avon. Turn right and stay on the track as it bends and then climbs to give good open views over the countryside. After about three quarters of a mile come into Stanton Drew and the main road.

2. STANTON DREW

For refreshment, turn right along the main road for a few yards to the Druids Arms. To contine our circle, turn left on the main road passing the small village war memorial and shortly, fork right and bend right again. Reach a sign for the famous Stone Circles, just to the left of the footpath which we are to take up the farm drive.

To visit the Stones, go left down a residential road and right at th end. There is an honesty box at the entrance for the £1 admission fee. Open 9am until sunset.

To continue, take the footpath up the farm drive. Go through a metal kissing gate and continue on the track, passing the main stone circles in the field left. Don't go through the next gate, but turn right along the field edge and go through anotherr metal kissing gate, ignoring a gate left. Now follow the hedge all the way to a road in Upper Stanton Drew.

3. SCHOOL

Turn left past the small village school and almot immediately go right on the marked footpath track just before Victoria Cottage. This brings you along through a kissing gate and into a field with a choice of paths. Stay in the field along the left hedge, heading for a metal kissing gate about half way along the far edge. If there are no crops in the field,you can bear right across the field to the gate. If planted, go round the left edge. Go through the gate and then carry on along the right hedge. Another kissing gate leads onto a road. Turn left past a line of houses. Ignore a first turn right by a phone box and continue to a right fork signed to Chelwood. Take this fork.

4. T-JUNCTION

Reach a T-junction. Go through the kissing gate opposite. Head across the field and over a plank bridge then climb up to trees atop a small hill. Cross a stile and go through the trees and drop down on the path. Maintain direction and go over a stile onto a

lane (Moorledge Lane). Cross over and uyp steps opposite, through a small gate, passing a house on the left. Go straight on along the grassy field edge in an area grazed by many horses. Ahead up on the hill are houses in Newton to where we are heading. Go through into the next field, crossing a small stream, and continue on along the left hedge climbing up to the road at the top.

5. ROAD

Here the route divides for a while. Route 1 takes you past the Pony and Trap pub and Route 2 goes across fields. Both meet at the foot of Knowle Hill.

Route 1: Turn right on the road shortly reaching the Pony and Trap which has an excellent garden out the back. Continue on and take the first road left, Knowle Hill. Follow this tarmac route round, ignoring a first footpath track and all other side turns. Rise gently, bend round and eventually find a footpath coming in on the left (the other route).On the right is a footpath going up onto the hill. Continue from *Knowle Hill.

Route 2: Go across the road and just at the start of Hollowbrook Lane go up steps on the right and through a gate. Turn left along the field edge. At a hedge corner, follow the footpath straight across the field. Turn left on the far side along the hedge. Reach a gate on the right and go into a field. Cross it, staying parallel with the left hedge and go through another gate by a large oak. Go through a wooded/scrubby area and reach the lane which circles the edge of Knowle Hill. See a footpath arrow more or less opposite. Follow the route from * Knowle Hill (below)

6. KNOWLE HILL*

Both routes join. Take the footpath up onto the hill and immediately fork right (if the path is passable, see below) and climb steeply to the top.

When the bracken and growth is at its height some of the paths in this Open Access Area are not clear but what you want to do for the best views is to get to the top and hopefully this path will be fine.

If not, don't fork up right but stay on the other path which climbs and then bends left, without reaching the top. Whatever you do, it is easy – you want to make for the far left side of the Knowle Hill area. If the path I mentioned is ok, reach the top and turn left on the ridge, walking with Chew Valley Lake down on the left and great views. There is a farm down right and Chew Magna is ahead in the distance at about 5 past the hour. Don't take any paths which drop down right. Continue more or less on, maybe bending slightly left and then begin the descent of the hill. It is a bridleway and may be a little muddy, after rain. The lower path I have just referred to, joins from the left. Maintain direction to the far boundary of the Knowle Hill area. Turn right with the hedge on left and continue to a house with an orange tiled roof.

7. HOUSE
Drop down left quite steeply and take the path down the left side of the house. Go through a gate, leaving the Open Access land, into a field and along the right edge. Cross a stile and pass converted stone houses on the right. Join the track leading to the houses and continue on. Later this joins an old track known as Pitts Lane. Continue on, going through a kissing gate, for well over half a mile to a lane.

8. LANE
Turn right a few yards and then climb left up steps. Turn right at the top of the bank to a gate and stile. Take the gate on the left and head down the right side of the field and into the next, drawing closer to Chew Magna. Bear down the centre of this field down to the far corner. Go through a gate, coming out by a cottage with a stream. Go right to a junction with a tarmac drive/lane. Turn left.

9. BRIDGES
Cross two bridges and go right on a path climbing up to the road in Chew Magna. Cross and turn right on the raised pavement past some of the fine old houses in the village – an attractive end to a really good walk.

Druids Arms, Stanton Drew, closed for lunch Mondays, 01275 332 230
Pubs and tea shop in Chew Magna.

Stepping back in time

From Wellow About 7 miles, 3.25 hours walking

OS Explorer Map 142, Shepton Mallet and Mendip Hills East, ref: 738 581

Refreshment: Tucker's Grave pub, or pub in Wellow

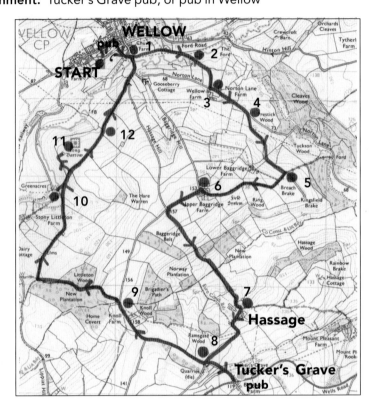

T HE quiet countryside of Mendip and North Somerset help to make this a tranquil and scenic circle from pretty Wellow, near Radstock.

Highlights include the unique, unspoilt pub at Tuckers Grave two-thirds of the way round, which is like stepping back in time. En route is a Neolithic chambered tomb, which you may have visited on another of my walks. There is also a great pub in Wellow.

TERRAIN: It's a circle of ups and downs, going through undulating 'horsey' country, and there are lovely changing views and contrasts of open scenery and woodland. Most of the circle is on dry paths and lanes although after rain there may be muddy and wet areas on the bridleways.

PARK: In the free car park in Wellow village, North East of Radstock. Wellow is off the A367 from the roundabout at Peasedown St John. The car park is signed off the village street on the right as you approach Wellow from this direction, just past the community village shop. It is down a turn on the right and situated on the site of the old station.

START: *Wellow was famous for its annual sheep fair in October throughout the c19th. Sadly, it ended during the First World War. The Somerset and Dorset Joint railway served the village well for over 90 years and closed in the Spring of 1966. It principally served to transport away processed Fullers' Earth, agricultural machinery, grain and watercress.*

Come out of the car park and turn right through Wellow with its beautiful stone houses.

By the phone box notice a red pig sculpture. He is one of 100 pigs in and around Bath sponsored, decorated and installed to raise money for the Two Tunnels project. This is one of three Wellow pigs and was designed by children from the Wellow playgroup and the art department of St Gregory's Catholic College, Odd Down. The pigs were due to be auctioned to raise money for the Two Tunnels project which involves burrowing under Combe Down to create a level and direct route between the centre of Bath and the Sustrans cycle route 2.5 miles south of the city.

Turn right at the Fox and Badger down Railway Lane, a pedestrian path. Pass the steam mill on the left and reach

the former Signal Box, now a home. Go straight ahead down the path in the valley and reach the Wellow Brook and ford and the late medieval packhorse bridge.

1. STREAM
Don't cross the stream. Simply, cross the lane and follow the footpath opposite over a stile. Walk ahead down the length of the field. There were many pheasant pens when we came here. Go through a metal gate. Bear right in field and follow the right fence. Ignore the first barrier/stile and fishermen's footbridge and continue along the fence to the next corner and cross a stile. Then go on and soon find a good metal footbridge over the water.

2. BRIDGE
Once over, follow the arrow bearing left up the field. There are pretty views over the valley as you rise. Go through a metal gate and up the next field, climbing. Cross a stile and follow the right-hand edge of the field – the footpath may be fenced off. A stile in the top corner leads onto a lane.

3. LANE
Turn left. The lane rises and as it levels out reach a marked bridleway on the right.

4. BRIDLEWAY
Go up it and under the power lines. At the pylon, turn left along the top edge of the field, in the heart of this pretty countryside. Bear right through a gate opening and continue in the same direction with a fence on your left. Go round the field corner and reach a metal hunting gate. Continue on and go through another gate and maintain direction along the left hedge. As you look back you can see Wellow church.

5. BY-WAY
Go onto a by-way and turn right up this old thoroughfare. After a few minutes you start to get a different view, left over the valley looking south. You can also get a good view of the White Horse on the down above Westbury.

6. FARM
The track reaches Lower Baggridge Farm. Go straight through onto a lane. Turn left, now walking along the top (at about 150 metres above sea level) with wide open views. Reach a lane coming from the right and opposite this turn left on the marked bridleway (the sign is up on the telegraph pole).
This next section was not well marked when I came here and the path was obscured by crops, but you may be luckier. The route goes straight ahead across the field keeping parallel with woodland over on your right and through a large gate (may well be open) on the far side into the next field. Maintain direction dropping down to the bottom hedge. Look for the gap into yet another field. Now continue descending following the left hedge.
In the bottom corner, go left onto a track and turn right on a track. Follow this along and uphill.

7. HASSAGE
Reach the hamlet of Hassage with several lovely old country homes, including Hassage Manor. Carry on through and join a lane. Reach a crossroads.

8. CROSSROADS
To visit Tuckers Grave Inn, turn left. The pub is three minutes away down on the corner.

This is a pub much acclaimed by CAMRA for its cider and ale and its unchanging nature. It has a great garden at the back and is very atmospheric inside, with no bar as such, but the barrels are under the window in the snug.
You should get a warm welcome from the landlord, Ivan Swift and his wife who have run it for a quarter of a century. When I came, there was a group of locals around one of the stripped pine tables enjoying the cider and a board of cheeses which they bring themselves each Sunday!
It was probably named after a local man,Edward Tucker who commited suicide in the mid c18th. It was the custom in those days for suicide victims to be buried in unhallowed ground, often at a remote crossroads such as the one here.

The pub serves simple sandwiches and rolls. (Groups should ring and order

barrow. Don't cross the bridge, but follow the sign right over a stile. And climb uphill along the top hedge.

11. LONG BARROW

*To visit the Barrow, reach a marked stile on the left. Cross this and follow the right hedge along the top of the field. Turn right over a stile and on across a small field and over another stile to come into the barrow area. Return to this point.

This is the very well preserved remains of a Neoloithic shrine or tomb with the burial chambers situated off a central gallery.

To continue our circle, continue uphill along the left hedge to a gate in the top corner. Maintain direction and pass the Long Barrow over on the left. Continue on and drop down.

12. HEDGED TRACK

Join a hedged track and follow this down – again, there my be muddy and wet patches along here. Reach a lane at the foot and turn left.
Soon return to the Wellow Brook, and old bridge where you were earlier. Cross and retrace your steps up the path back to the Fox and Badger. Then it's left back to the village car park.

The Fox and Badger, Wellow, 01225 832293
Tucker's Grave Inn, 01373 834230

beforehand).
Return to the crossroads you came from and carry straight on, climbing for a while. (If not visiting the pub, you turn right at the crossroads.) Ignore a left turn and a bridleway.

9. COTTAGE

After about three quarters of a mile from the pub, pass a cottage and turn left along the far side on a by-way. This may be a little muddy. The track takes you through woodland and when you come into the open reach a track junction.
Turn right. Follow this gently up and at the next junction of tracks, keep straight on along the top of the hill with great views across the Wellow valley, following the right hedge.
Pass a ruined barn and start to drop downhill. A track comes in from the left. Ignore this and continue straight over and down hill.

10. WOODEN FOOTBRIDGE

Just before the Wellow Brook and a large wooden footbridge, there is a metal marker for the Ancient Monument of the Stony Littleton Long

Photos from the walks in this book

On the right track

From Mells. About 4.5 miles, 2.5 hours walking.

OS Explorer Map 142, Shepton Mallet & Mendip Hills East, ref: 727 492

Refreshment: Pub in Mells

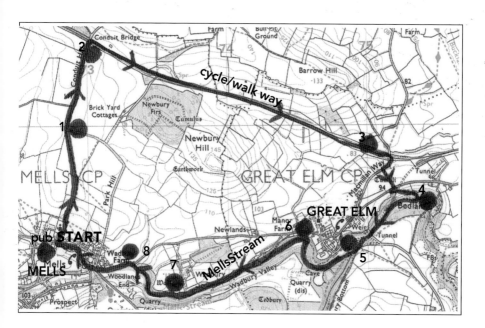

T his gentle circle is 'a plum' walk in the Eastern Mendips in more ways than one and a new twist on one I have written before in this area. It can now be completed by using the Colliers Way, a good dry walking track on the old railway through the beautiful countryside. We then cross to a deep rugged river valley where undergrowth hides evidence of an amazing industrial past. The area is now a rich haven for wildlife. In Mells is a very popular pub, the Talbot.

TERRAIN: The route is flat with virtually no stiles but gives the

chance for good fast walking along the old railway line to get your energy flowing. Bring your dog.

PARK: in the village of Mells about three miles west of Frome. Find somewhere safe near the Talbot Inn.

START: *Mells is forever linked with the old nursery rhyme of little Jack Horner. One version is that Jack was a scullion in the Abbey Kitchen of Glastonbury at a time when Mells was owned by the Abbot. He, in an effort to save his property at the time of the dissolution of the monasteries, sent the deeds to a place of security, hidden in a pie, and* entrusted to Jack Horner. Being hungry, the boy promptly opened the pie and discovered 'the plum' - the deeds, and thus became the owner. It's a good story, but untrue as, Mells was bought from Henry VIII by Thomas Horner and the legal deeds proving this were preserved.

Turn up the street at the side of the Talbot Inn.

This is New Street designed in 1470 by Abbot Selwood of Glastonbury Abbey and was meant to be the start of a town plan in the shape of a cross, but only New Street was ever completed.

Go through to the fine c15th church.

It contains much fine work by a number of artists who were friends of the Horner family, the Lords of the Manor of Mells who lived next door. The works include including a stained

glass window by William Nicholson.

Walk outside the church to the right.

In the churchyard on your right is a simple grave of the renowned poet, Siegfried Sassoon who died in 1967 and was buried here beside Ronald Knox, the distinguished RC priest and scholar who lived in Mells Manor while translating the Bible.

Leave the churchyard round the back up the eye-catching avenue of clipped yews designed by Edward Lutyens.

Go up the field and through a gate to the next field. Go straight across the field to a gap in the hedge and in the next field head for the far left corner (go round the edge if there are crops). Make sure you ignore a stile in the corner on the way.

1. LANE
In the far corner come on to Conduit Lane. Go left (straight ahead in reality) and after a few minutes come to Conduit Bridge.

2. COLLIERS WAY
Go down onto the walk and cycle track, the Colliers Way.

The Colliers Way is part of the National Cycle Network, that will eventually run from Dundas, near Bath to Southampton and this section follows the route of the old GWR Radstock to Frome Branch Line.

Turn right under the bridge and continue on for about 1.5 miles passing on the way one or two benches and picnic tables. The old

Go up and across the field to the far side to a fence/stile onto the road. Cross with care. Turn right and shortly go left down a No Through lane to the Mells Stream.

4. MELLS STREAM
Turn right over the stream and then right through a kissing gate onto a path which runs alongside the fast-flowing river so much the life blood of Mells. Immediately on the right you will see the remains of an old mill in the stream.

In Spring the valley is a mass of snowdrops and later with violets and monkshood .

Go under the railway bridge and on, passing in a few minutes a beautiful converted mill house. Follow the stream all the way to the road by the bridge at Great Elm.

5. GREAT ELM
Cross the road and go straight over following the track opposite. After a few yards at the gate leading to the railway line, turn right down over a stile and over the stream. The path divides. Turn right. This path goes across and picks up the main Mells Stream again, bending left. You are walking with the water on your right along rugged wooded Wadbury Valley.

6. BRIDGE
Cross right over the first bridge and then turn left and continue along with the Mells Stream on your left.

rails are still in place as you will see alongside the track.   Be alert for cyclists along here and make sure your dog is under control.
  You go through a metal gate on the way and over a cattle grid and just continue on. Pass English apple trees planted at intervals.

Artists worked on this project with local schools to develop the concept of a 'Linear Orchard' which was planted by Sustrans. The orchard consists of English apple trees planted at intervals to highlight disappearing orchards in Somerset, and echo self seeded fruit trees (from apple cores thrown from trains).

The track drops gently downhill.

3. INFORMATION BOARD
  Reach a large and detailed informa-tion board about the Colliers Way, just before a railway bridge. Here you don't continue on under the bridge, but leave the track and go up onto a lane. Turn right, climbing gently. Very shortly, take the first gate on the left.

The whole valley is a green and secretive confusion of undergrowth hiding remains of the former famous Fussells of Mells, edge tool industry. Eventually, the path becomes tarmac for a while and you go through a lawn area with houses up on the right. Continue on, following the footpath which hugs the stream (don't go up the drive). Before long reach old walls on your left and the first signs of what was the main iron works.

7. RUINS
There are glimpses through the crumbling walls of what was once an immense industrial site.

If you carry on to the end of the long high wall you may be able to turn left down into the site. Take care as there are many deep pits and unsafe crumbling masonry and please respect any warning or no entry signs.

From the mid c18th until the end of the c19th workers toiled under 'the iron rule' of the Fussells' family to make the name of Fussells of Mells

known throughout the Empire. At the height, there were between 400-500 people working at probably six sites along here. They produced edge-tools such as hay knives, scythes, billhooks spades, shovels.
The demise of English agriculture in the 1870s began the downfall of Fussells. By 1895 all production had ended. Now nature has taken over.

8. ROAD
Come out onto the road. Turn left. Continue to a junction where over on the left is a memorial by Lutyens to Mark Horner - a Community Water Tap and Shelter.
Go ahead on the Coleford Road.

At the next junction is a Lutyens' designed War Memorial where every-one, regardless of rank or social standing, is listed alphabetically.

Continue on, passing a fine c15th tithe barn left, now used as a village hall. Continue on to the Talbot and the start.

The Talbot Inn, Mells, 01373 812254

Along the old canal
From Highbridge (Coleford).
About 5.25 miles, 2.45 hours walking
Explorer OS 142 map, Shepton Mallet & Mendip Hills East, ref: 685494

Refreshment: Pubs at Edford and Holford

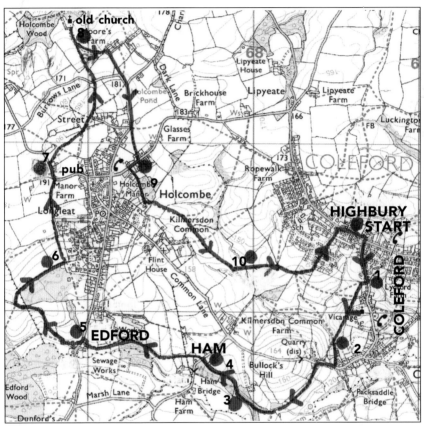

A peaceful, easy circle through the attractive rolling countryside of East Mendip visiting an old church and following the route of the ill fated Dorset and Somerset Canal. There is glorious woodland as well as open fields. En route, just over half way, is a very welcoming country inn.

TERRAIN: Undulating country with no big hills. There are stiles and kissing gates but they could be managed by dogs, even non agile ones!

PARK: in the British Legion car park at Highbury – the northern suburb of Coleford. Coleford is an old mining village equi-distant from Shepton Mallet, Frome and Radstock. The Legion has kindly given us parking permission, but make sure you park well out of the way.

START: Turn left from the car park for a few yards. At the crossroads turn right towards Leigh on Mendip. Go downhill and as the houses end on the left reach a crossing footpath.

1.PATH

Turn right on the path between a house and garage and go into a field. Turn left along the top edge and on into the next field, with pretty views down on the right across the valley and Kilmersdon Common. Maintain direction. At the hill edge, go through a kissing gate and steeply down to a narrow valley.

2. VALLEY

Turn left and follow the path which then bends and goes under a brick arch.

This is an old aqueduct known locally as the 'hucky duck' - the largest of the works completed on the ill-fated Dorset and Somerset Canal designed to serve local collieries and join up with the Somerset Coal Canal.

Reach the drive to a house and turn left soon coming to the road. Turn

right uphill until you reach a marked footpath on the left through a gate, passing to the left of a wooden garage. Go over a metal barrier and on on to a kissing gate into a field. Turn right paralleling the right hedge. The valley of the Mells Stream is down on your left. Go into woodland.

3. OLD CANAL

You are now following the old canal towpath through the woods – the canal bed is down on your right. On the other side of the wood, continue on. Just maintain your direction now, crossing several stiles, going through more woodland and on until a path brings you to a lane.

4. HAM

This is the edge of the hamlet of Ham. Cross the stile opposite and continue on in the same direction as before through similar countryside – wood-

land and open areas - and shadowing the old canal for a while, before it disappears, The path can be quite winding and undulating and has a few steps in places. Ignore any side turns and try and stay roughly in the same direction on the main path.

Leave the woodland and go ahead through a field, along the left fence,through a kissing gate and reach a crossing track. The footpath used to go ahead through the garden to the main road, but is in the process of being diverted. So you may well need to go right on the track and then left to the main road in Edford.

5. EDFORD

Turn left down the main road. Then shortly, reach a stile on the right.(For a very short detour, there is the Duke of Cumberland a little further down the road but you need to ring to see if they are serving lunches. Cross the stile and go ahead in the field.

As you go, see the bricked up arch of the old canal bridge. On the other side was the Edford holding basin where boats waited to continue their journey.

Cross onto a track and turn right. Go through a kissing gate and on through woodland, climbing gently. Then leave the woodland and continue ahead on a track. When woodland ends on your right, cross right over a stile. Cross the field corner, go over a stile and hug woodland on your right. Negotiate another stile and continue.

6. POND

Reach a pond. A footbridge leads into another field. Go on to about the centre and then turn up to the top

hedge where you will find a stile next to a metal gate about half way along. There are good views behind at this point. Cross and bear across to the right hedge near houses and continue up, to cross a stile in the top corner. Go on in the next field to another stile in the top corner near three copper beeches. Go ahead along the left fence and over a metal bar stile on the far side. Turn left on the lane and start to see Downside Abbey.

7. PUB

Reach the restored Holford Inn.

This was formerly the Ring o' Roses country pub - the name was a reminder of the Plague that destroyed the old Holcombe village.
The Inn has a glorious garden and an imaginative menu.

Go on a few yards and cross right over a stile hidden in the hedge. Head straight up across the field to the top left corner. Maintain direction, going over the stile ahead with two arrows on it (not left) and follow the left hedge for a short distance to a stile on the left. Cross and bear right across the field corner towards a cottage. Stay in the field and bear left passing to the side of the cottage on

your right. There is a good view of Downside Abbey. A stile leads onto a lane. Take the stile opposite and cross the field to the far side. Cross another stile and head straight across and down to a metalled lane/drive.

8. CHURCH DRIVE
To visit Holcombe Old Church turn left, although the church is kept locked. But it is a peaceful spot.

The original medieval village here was buried at the time of the Plague. In more modern times, Scott of the Antartic's parents lived in Holcombe, in Holcombe Manor, and there is a family grave behind the church on the left.

To continue, go back up the lane/drive, through a farm and on, ignoring a right turn. Join the main road. Turn right. After about three minutes, at a bend, go left over a stile on the marked path near a playground sign. Go across small paddocks and over stiles in the same direction. Then cross a stile by a gate near a house.

9. ROAD
Go out onto the road and turn right.

Shortly, turn left down the drive to Hill House. At the open area at the end, take the marked path left through a kissing gate and walk along a wide fenced path. Go into another field and on along the fence which soon bends right. In the corner go through a metal gate. Go straight over the mound in the field ahead and then on, gradually bearing left to trees below.

10. STREAM
Cross the stream footbridge. Head up the field. At the top, go ahead over a stile and then bear right across the field. Go into another field and follow the left hedge. About half way along go left through a kissing gate into woodland. Take the right fork and reach houses on the edge of Coleford. Go between them and reach a cul-de-sac by garages. Go straight out and left on the access road. At the main road, turn right to the British Legion car park.

The Duke of Cumberland, Edford 01761 232412
The Holford Inn, open daily for lunch, tel: Tel 01761 232478

Beacon Wood beckons

From Chelynch About 5 miles, 2.5 hours walking

OS Explorer Map 142, Shepton Mallet and Mendip Hills East, ref: 648 439

Refreshment: Pub at Chelynch

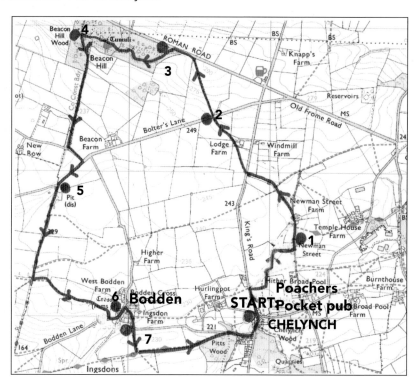

THIS gentle East Mendip circle starts from the hamlet of Chelynch, east of Shepton Mallet, crosses farmland and uses quiet lanes to reach ancient Beacon Wood renowned for bluebells and historic interest. Then the old Fosse Way, the East Mendip Way and field paths take us back to the start and a welcoming pub.

TERRAIN: A couple of gentle hills but mainly the going is on the flat. Wear good shoes or boots, as usual. It's a good walk for well-behaved dogs with

a number of wooden and stone stiles but most dogs should be able to negotiate these.

PARK: The hamlet of Chelynch, just north of Doulting and east of Shepton Mallet. The landlord of the popular Poachers Pocket has given permission for walkers to use his car park, but asks that you let him know. It's a great pub for drinks and refreshment.

START: Turn left out of the car park and walk down the lane at the side. Shortly, reach a crossing footpath and go up right over a stone stile and follow the footpath (the East Mendip Way) across the field. At the stile on the far side, don't cross, but stay in the field and go left along the edge. Go round the first corner for a few yards and then cross right over a stone stile. In this next field follow the right edge round one corner and reach the first kissing gate on the right. Go through and down the left edge coming out through another kissing gate onto a quiet lane on the edge of the small hamlet of Newman Street.

1. HAMLET
Turn left on the lane for over a third of a mile and reach a junction with a small country road. Cross the stile opposite and go across the field bearing right towards the left side of a farm. Cross a stile and then another on the other side of the concrete farm track. Now follow the right fence to a stile in the corner. Once over, follow the arrow across the field, slightly left, to a tall stone slab stile and come onto a lane.

2. LANE
Go over the stile opposite and head uphill in this large field to the top left corner by woodland. There are good views across the Levels and Glastonbury Tor. Cross the stile near the top corner and come onto the busy road, originally an old Roman route across Mendip. Turn left and walk along the edge with care. In a couple of minutes reach an entrance to Beacon Wood on the left.

3. BEACON WOOD
The wood is a prominent landscape feature visible for miles in many directions. It is owned by the Woodland Trust and managed by a local group, the Beacon Society, which has a woodland management plan to encourage native species. With ponds, rides and glades of bluebells, it is a wood of contrasts. Beacon Wood is also important from an archaeological point of view with many features dating from the Neolithic, Bronze Age and Roman periods right through to the present day. It is an Open Access area so you are free to wander and explore.

Follow the main path through the woods. After six minutes reach a grassy swathe/track on the left (a few yards before a track going right to a gate onto the road). Go left on this and soon come to two mature beech trees. Pass them and then bear right up to the mound topped by a stone pillar, giving the place a Pagan feel. Go past the pillar and continue on in the same direction through the wood, coming across various tumuli. Reach a smaller pillar, dated 1766.

This marks the junction of four parishes. You can see two of the parish names still carved – Shepton and Doulting.

Eventually reach the main crossing track - the old Roman Road, the Fosse Way. (If you look to the right you can see another entrance gate on the main road.)
Our route goes left down the track. But for a small diversion and good views, go more or less straight over onto a level dry path to an unusual large wooden seat, ideal for a picnic.

It was erected in memory of the

pioneer of the Beacon Society, Fraser Townend.

4. FOSSE WAY 1
Return to the sunken ancient track and follow it along and downhill. It bends and eventually leaves the wood. The track now heads straight out between trees and leads all the way to a lane. Turn left.
At a road junction, turn right and after a few minutes at a very slight bend, turn left on a track – returning, in fact, to the old Fosse Way.

5. FOSSE WAY 2
This soon passes an old quarry left, climbs gently and gives pleasant views over fields and woods.
After just under half a mile, ignore one marked footpath on the left (arrow on gate) and shortly after this on the left reach a gate and stone stile (opposite a metal gate and stile on the right). Cross and head across the field to the corner jutting out and continue on to the far edge, but bearing away to the right. Aim for a stile to the left of a clump of beeches in the hedgeline. Go over into another field. It may not be marked here. Make your way across the field towards the hamlet of Bodden, bearing very slightly right. Cross a stile and immediately another one. Bear to the right down the field, passing to the left of a cottage. Leave through a large metal gate.

6. BODDEN
Turn left on the lane and come into Bodden, a small farming community. Turn right at the first junction and pass a large farm. At a left bend, leave the lane.

7. FARM TRACK
Go straight ahead through a gate and up a concrete farm track, climbing gently up Ingsdons Hill and getting a good view across Shepton Mallet. Keep on all the way to a junction of gates.
Go through a wooden kissing gate on the left, rejoining the East Mendip Way. Follow the right hedge, looking across on the right to Doulting and its distinctive church. Cross a stone stile in the corner and continue as before along the right hedge. In the next corner, cross another stile and go down onto a lane. Turn right and follow this along, past a pond, and up to a junction in Chelynch.
Turn left back to the Poachers Pocket, a good traditional local serving real ales and cider and a range of tempting good value food.

The Poachers Pocket, Chelynch, 01749 880220

31

A wander from Wells

From Wells. About 6.25 miles, 3 hours walking.

OS Explorer Map 141, Cheddar Gorge & Mendip Hills West , ref: 551 457

Refreshment: Pubs in Croscombe. A big choice in Wells, of course.

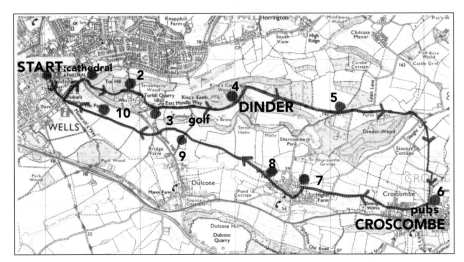

A PLEASANT circle from Wells taking in the East Mendip Way and the high ridge to the east. So it includes the beautiful city of Wells, two traditional Somerset villages and the countryside around. The circle follows footpaths through fields and woods. The last leg across 'the park' , the open land, beyond the Bishop's Palace gives great views of the cathedral.

TERRAIN: Easy walking with only one short climb near the start. Footpaths through woods and fields and quiet lanes are mainly dry underfoot. A good walk at any time of year.

PARK: Find somewhere suitable In Wells. There are a number of public car parks.

START: In front of the main door of Wells Cathedral with your back to the door. Turn left and go through the small arch, the Penniless Porch, towards the market square. Turn immediately left towards the Bishop's Palace. Follow the moat on your left and then round left. Continue until you leave through a barrier onto a road.

Cross the road, and take the track/ lane more-or-less opposite. Go along for about 50 yards and turn right up steps on the East Mendip Way.

1. EAST MENDIP WAY
Look for the Way's green disc.

The East Mendip Way is an 18 -mile linear walk from Wells to Frome and can be linked with the West Mendip

Way from Uphill near Weston-super-Mare to Wells. They form a challenging trek through varying landscape.

Continue to climb, avoiding side paths and reach a gate leading into an open field.

2. FIELD

Go straight across and enter woodland again. Follow the path which bends and leads out into open land again. Continue on with Tor Hill works and quarry on your right. Go down the length of the grassy stretch and then bend round right and continue to follow the quarry fence and woodland on your right. Come into another open area and go straight down the centre. In the far right corner, cross a stone slab stile.

3. STONE STILE

Turn left on the track. It's not long before you come alongside the golf course. Then the path begins to climb gently up by King's Castle Wood.

This is a nature reserve in the care of Somerset Wildlife Trust. It's an ancient wood - mainly oak and ash leading up to an Iron Age Hillfort, and home to many interesting plants, including wood goldilocks, birds, including tawny owls and buzzards, and animals such as roe deer and badgers.

The path divides. Make sure you stay on the upper one which goes up through a gate. Go up quite steeply into a field. Turn right on the crossing track through a beautiful green oasis surrounded by glorious woodland. Go through a small band of woodland and on through the open land again to the very far end.

4. GATE

Go through a wooden gate and ahead on a lane/track. Shortly, turn right on the East Mendip Way through a gate. Walk down the full length, passing a brick pillbox on the right. In the far right corner, go through a gate and continue in the same direction on a track. Drop down and come into an open area. When the trees on the right end, go right up the bank and into a field. Go straight across the field to a stile by a metal gate leading to a lane.

5. LANE
Cross and take the track opposite which shortly brings you to dilapidated corrugated iron sheds. Turn right over a stile and cross a field. A metal kissing gate on the far side brings you to another field. Head across in the same direction as before, getting good views across Somerset and including Glastonbury Tor. Cross a stile and continue on down. A gate leads onto a track. Turn left for a few yards and then cross right over a stile with a great view of Croscombe below. Go straight down through two fields and over a stile in the bottom left corner of the second field and come onto a road called the Fayreway at the top of Croscombe.

6. CROSCOMBE
For the village and pubs turn left and then right down Church Street.

The large church is of particular interest, having an unusual spire for Somerset, and Jacobean interior woodwork of National renown.

The Bull Terrier is at the foot of the street, with the old Market Cross outside, and the George a few yards right from there along the main road.

Croscombe is a unique and interesting little village nestling in a Mendip valley by the River Sheppey. It was not until after the Great Plague and the subsequent boom in the wool trade in the $c16^{th}$ and $c17^{th}$ that Croscombe really emerged. Many significant houses, cottages and hostelries were built and many still survive. Following the decline of the wool trade and the impact of the Industrial Revolution, silk, mining, quarrying and milling all left their mark on the village landscape.

To continue, return to the Fayreway. and go past houses and the village hall. On the bend by a postbox, cross a stile and go across the field, over another stile and on along the side of the valley. In the corner a stile brings you to another field. Maintain direction. You can see Dinder ahead. Cross a stile and lane and follow the path on, going over a stile by a gate. Go into the next field and past a farm. Go over a stone stile on the far side and on to reach a kissing gate ahead. Go out onto a lane in Dinder.

7. DINDER
Go left and at the junction go straight on and soon pass Dinder church.

The lychgate and resting house for coffins are notable, as is the ancient twisted yew (one book suggests it is over 1,200 years old) on the south

side of the church.
The squire of Dinder in Victorian times, Squire Somerville, used to line up his estate staff to pay them on Fridays and asked if each man had been to church on the previous Sunday. If the answer was 'yes', the worker was given an extra half crown. Thus the term 'half crown Christians' grew up.
Pretty Dinder nestles in a valley - the name, in fact, means 'in a deep valley between high hills'. It had a thriving cottage clothing industry in the c18th with its own leather mill.

Carry on past the church. At the end enter a field on the Wells footpath.

8. RECREATION GROUND
Go round the right edge of the recreation ground and take the kissing gate to the left of the pavilion. Head to the far right corner of the next field and near the corner cross a stile. Follow the right hedge. When it kinks, go right through a gate and then left. Don't enter the field ahead, but instead turn right along the hedge and follow it round the corner and continue along the bottom edge of the field. Go over a stile and cross the next field, passing to the left of an oak. Take the stile by a gate and cross a track.

9. TRACK
Cross another stile and follow the left hedge. Go on into the next field and on to cross the road. Take the foopath opposite and go up through a metal gate onto a tarmac path. Soon see Wells Cathedral ahead.

10. THE PARK
This path continues on, going through 'the Park' - the open park-like fields by the Cathedral and Bishop's Palace - through one or two gates, all the way to Wells. Come out by the corner of the moat round the Bishop's Palace. Go straight back to the start.

The Bull Terrier, 01749 343658; The George,01749 342306, both at Croscombe

Walk ten

Enchanting Ebbor

From Ebbor Gorge Nature Reserve, above Wookey Hole
About 3.25 miles, 1.5 hours walking
Explorer OS 142 map, Shepton Mallet & Mendip Hills East, ref: 685 494

Refreshment: Pub and cafes in Wookey Hole

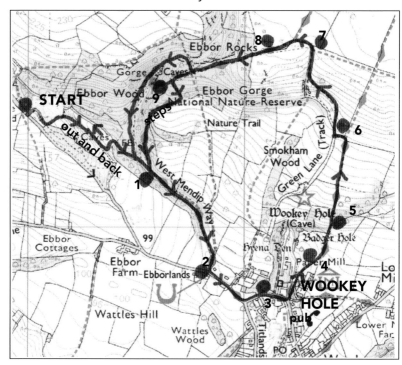

This short but strenuous circle is one of the loveliest on Mendip in Ebbor Gorge National Nature Reserve just above Wookey Hole. High up on a rocky edge in the heart of this limestone Gorge is one of the best viewpoints in Mendip. It's a wonder at any time of year with good bluebells in spring. Expect to see wildflowers, butterflies and plenty of birdlife, too...so take your binoculars (you may see Peregrine Falcons). En route is Wookey Hole with its attractions. Dogs should be kept on leads in the Gorge.

TERRAIN: There are two steep climbs and the option of a dramatic scramble down through the actual narrow gorge or an easier steps route. Be sure to wear stout shoes or boots with grips especially if you choose the Gorge scramble.

PARK: In the National Trust Ebbor Gorge car park. Go in the top entrance sited up the lane from Wookey Hole leading onto Mendip and Priddy. At the side of the car park is a National Trust information kiosk. Wookey Hole lies to the North West of Wells.

START: Cross a stone slab stile in the top corner of the car park into the wooded Gorge area. We are following the red route for a while and going steeply down steps. At a marker post, turn left deeper into the Reserve. Cross a small stream/ditch and bend round and continue on the path. Reach another marker and go right (no longer on the red route).

1. STEPS

Reach steps going up left. Avoid these – you will be coming down these at the end. Simply, stay down, following the path along the bottom, avoiding side turns. (We will be walking up higher in the Gorge towards the end of our walk.) Leave the wooded Gorge through a gate and continue through a grassy valley. Go to the very far end and bend round to follow a path out to the lane on the edge of Wookey Hole.

2. LANE

Turn left into the village, ignoring a lane on the right.

3. WOOKEY HOLE

Here is the famous Wookey Hole cave, papermill and other tourist attractions. There are a number of cafes in the village and the popular Wookey Hole Inn a little further on.
To start the shorter journey back take the lane to the right side of the Paper Mill (facing the mill) School Hill. Climb up the lane and at a bend at the top by the nursing home car park go straight ahead through a gate on the Monarch's Way.

4. MONARCH'S WAY

This is a 610-mile footpath following as closely as possible the epic escape of Charles II after the Battle of Worcester - through the Midlands south and on to Bridport, then across the South Downs to Shoreham, where a boat was found to take him to France.

Turn right up the fence and follow the grassy track on. It then curves gently left across the field to where there is an indent in the woodland.

5. STILE

Here you will find a stile to cross under the trees. Go straight ahead, climbing up the field steeply and go through a gap at the top into another field, and continue on and up. On the far side is another stile. Take time to look at the wonderful views unfolding behind. Once over the stile, maintain your direction across this field, which is virtually flat! Cross yet another stile on the far side, by a very ancient oak.

Ignore the sign going straight ahead. Instead turn left into the next field and then continue on, contouring round the hill and very gradually bending right and climbing.

6. TRACK

Pick up a track and follow it on up through gorse, brambles, and bushes. Down on your left are the woods of Ebbor Gorge. Eventually come up out into the open. Head up to the top, just past a metal gate which is face on to you, and find a stile on the left in the actual corner.

7. TOP

Cross left over the stile and continue along the top of the field to the next corner with great views over the Levels. In the corner turn left following the right fence and continue on to a stile and gate ahead.

8. EBBOR GORGE

Cross the stile ahead, entering back into Ebbor Gorge Reserve. Continue on down and cross another stile to bring you onto a path into the woodland. Soon reach a low marker post at a small crossroads of paths. Here there is a choice – either going steeply down the actual Gorge with a short scramble, or going down the many stepped path. But which ever route, it is worth going on for a short way to the wonderful viewpoint. So after about 125 yards straight on,

see the sign for the viewpoint.

9. VIEWPOINT

Take care, not to go too close to the edge if you are a bit nervous about heights. It is a sunny rocky and grassy vantage point where you can quietly stand or sit and soak up the views - very uplifting.

For the stepped route continue on the path past the viewpoint and follow the steps down to the bottom, where you passed by earlier. Turn right, passing a bench made from half a log and reach a marker post for the red route path from the Gorge. Here both routes join at *MARKER POST..

For the actual Gorge route - for those who are fit and sure of their footing: from the viewpoint go back to the low marker post and turn left downhill. At the foot, turn left and just follow this path on down, going through a rocky, steep section where you will have to scramble and just continue on down, ignoring side turns. It's very beautiful quiet route and gives you a good feel of the dramatic nature of the Gorge. Reach a marker post (back to front) and maintain direction. Reach a junction with another track. You came by here earlier. Here the stepped route joins.

*9. MARKER POST

If coming from the Gorge, turn right. If coming from the stepped route bend left. Follow the path along and retrace your steps of earlier. In case you have forgotten - further on, turn right and continue up and along and steeply up steps back to the car park.

The Wookey Hole Inn, 01749 676677

Can you spot where these were taken?

Doing your level best

From Westhay Moor About 6 miles, 3 hours walking

OS Explorer 141, Cheddar Gorge & Mendip Hills West, ref: 455 437

Refreshment: Pub at Lower Godney. Two options for tea nearby

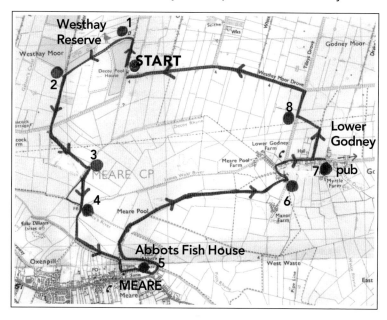

THE big skies, abundant bird life, rhynes, ponds and peat moors of the Somerset Levels between the Mendips and the Polden Hills combine to make this a memorable, interesting and flat circle. We walk in the area of the former ancient Lake Villages and take in Westhay Moor Nature Reserve and the c14th Abbots Fish House at Meare, once an island community, as well as a riverside pub. Keep dogs well under control and take your binoculars for bird watching.

TERRAIN: Walking is on tracks and lanes and across the flat fields, grazed by cattle. There are one or two sections which may be churned up by animals and muddy. The fields on the Levels can get wet after a prolonged period of rain.

PARK: In the free car parking area at Westhay Moor Nature Reserve. Take the B3151 road south from Wedmore to Glastonbury and about 3 miles out of Wedmore turn left on a bend at a low Turnpike House on a side road marked to Godney and Glastonbury. After about 1.2 miles, at a sharp right bend, turn left into a parking area divided off by large boulders. There is a Westhay Moor Reserve board on the left as you turn off the road.

START: Before you start, take time to look at the Reserve's information board.

It is an unusual place - almost a hybrid of land and sea. The 250 acre reserve is managed by the Somerset Wildlife Trust which started to get involved in 1970. At that time the landscape had been severely damaged by industrial peat cutting and agriculture. The area is home to otters, dragonflies and carnivorous sundew plants - a red, moss-like growth which dissolve hapless insects. Of course, it is also visited by over wintering and migratory birds. A spectacular sight is the annual arrival of up to eight million starlings who take refuge in the reed beds.

Walk away from the road along the track between ponds and reed beds in an area created out of the old peat workings. Take the first marked path into the Reserve on the left through a gate towards a large bird hide.

1. HIDE
Go to the left of the hide and continue along the grassy track, ignoring all gates and side turns. Go quietly so that you stand the best chance of seeing birds and wild life. Maintain direction until you reach a gate ahead onto a wide crossing drove.

2. DROVE
Turn left and the drove leads to the road. Cross over onto a track opposite between rhynes. Shortly, take the first marked footpath on the left through a large metal gate into a field. It may be somewhat muddy along here if cattle or farm machinery have been

around. Head across under the power lines, keeping the pylon over on your right. Go through a gate and cross a rhyne and maintain direction heading for a modern barn, with Glastonbury Tor in the distance behind.

3. BARN
Cross a bridge to the barn and go through the yard. Go to the right of the barn and into the field. Go down with the rhyne on your right. Go over a low stone bridge into another field. You can either bear diagonally across the field heading for a large foot-bridge over a rhyne on the far side, or simply continue to follow the rhyne on your right until you reach a crossing rhyne. Then turn left along it. Both routes should bring you to a visible and well constructed wooden foot-bridge.

4. BRIDGE
Cross the footbridge and continue on with a rhyne on your left and in the corner, go left through a metal gate. Now bear diagonally left, cutting across the corner of the field, to the River Brue on the far side.

Not far from here were the Lake Villages of Meare, dating from third and second centuries BC. Excavations showed that it was a highly skilled and prosperous community. The marsh settlements were built on artificial foundations of logs, brush-wood, clay and rubble laid down systematically on the edge of the open water. Today only slight mounds are visible where once the villages stood. At Meare there were two settlements, each of about 60 dwell-ings It appears that the people grew grain and kept cattle and sheep, practising a wide range of crafts and industries and were quite prosperous compared with similar settlements. The Peat Moors Visitor Centre near Westhay can tell you more.

Then turn left along the river edge all the way to a stone footbridge near Meare. Go through the metal gate ahead at the bridge.
Cross the bridge and continue on towards a farm and the church behind. Go through a wide metal gate and along the side of the farmyard, through another gate and then bend left with the church wall on your right. There is a path on the right that leads to the church entrance.

Abbot Adam of Sodbury built the church here in the decorated style in the early c14th.

To continue, pass in front of impressive c14th Manor Farm and then go left on the far side and immediately turn right through a wooden gate. Cross the field to the Abbots Fish House.

5. FISH HOUSE
The only surviving monastic fishery building in England, this housed the Abbot of Glastonbury's water bailiff and was used for fish-salting and drying. It used to be on the banks of Meare Pool which teemed with fish providing food for the monks of Glastonbury Abbey. The Fish House was also a storage for salted or smoked fish.
It is thought to have been built at about the same time as the Manor House when Adam de Sodbury was Abbott between 1322 and 1335.

Continue on past it along a stone slab path and out of a gate onto a lane by the main road. Turn left on the lane which leads to a bridge over the Brue. Cross and then turn left along the bank and go through gates until you come back to the stone bridge where you turned off for the church. Don't go through the metal gate onto the end of the bridge, but instead bear ahead down to the right across the field to a gate in the far corner by a rhyne. Go through the gates and continue on with the rhyne on your left to a junction of rhynes. Go through a wooden gate over one rhyne and then cross left over a bridge. Turn right along the edge of a rhyne keeping it on your right and reach a pill box.

5. PILL BOX
Drop down to the left and continue to a rusty metal gate, marked with a footpath arrow (ignore a metal gate on the right). Walk along with a hedged rhyne on your right through two large fields. Enter a third field and turn right. Go on into the field at the side and follow a farm track left which takes you to a farm on the edge of Lower Godney.

On the right of the village is an interesting white round house which you can see closer up later.

6. FARM

Go through onto a lane in Lower Godney. To see the round house, make a short detour to the right along the lane and then return here.

It is a weekend and holiday dwelling of straw, wood and lime with a grass clad roof .

To continue, turn left. At a junction near a phone box, turn right. Continue to another junction and go straight on. After passing the entrance to the village hall, arrive at a marked footpath on the left. Our walk continues along here. But for the Sheppey Inn, go on a few more yards.

7. PUB

It has an attractive riverside decking patio and is noted for reasonably-priced meals and snacks.

Go back to the footpath. Follow it on over a footbridge and stile and go ahead in two fields keeping the hedge on your right. In the third field, bear diagonally left, going under power lines, to a large metal gate onto the road near the far corner.

8. ROAD

Turn right and now enjoy great views of the southern edge of the Mendip ridge as you go. When you reach the first junction, turn left and follow this fairly quiet road, passing alongside ponds and former peat workings for just over a mile, back to the car park.

● After the walk you can have tea at Sweet's Tea Rooms - just round the corner on the road to Wedmore - or drive into Lower Godney and on to Upper Godney to Annie's Tea Rooms, serving delicious organic food - lunches and teas or just a good coffee or tea and a homemade cake. (open Easter to end of Sept).

The Sheppey Inn tel: 01458 832917 Annies's Tea Rooms, Upper Godney, tel: 01458 832547.

A yew and views

From the ridge south of Street, near Marshalls Elm Junction.
6.25 miles, about 3 hours walking. (Can be shortened).
OS Explorer Map 141 Cheddar Gorge & Mendip Hills West,
ref: 480 344
Refreshment: Pub at Compton Dundon

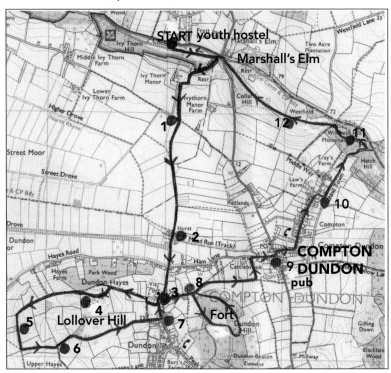

THERE is a 1,750-year-old yew tree at the heart of this wonderful circular ramble in Somerset near Street from the eastern edge of the Polden Ridge.

Its an area that many believe has a special tranquillity and mysticism, much like Glastonbury Tor. The loop over Lollover Hill is optional. Then the walk skirts Dundon Hill and Dundon Beacon which you can climb if you wish, and in early summer expect to see many species of orchids on both

hills. In the village of Compton Dundon there's a welcoming pub. After that, continue up to the Hood Monument followed by a beautiful ridge walk with fantastic views.

TERRAIN: There are two or three hills and moderate walking on good paths. A suitable dog outing.

PARK: At NT's Ivythorne Hill parking area by the the road opposite the Youth Hostel, south of Street. Take the B3151 Street- Somerton Road and at Marshalls Elm junction turn right on the Ashcott road. The parking lay-by is a short way along. Or use the car park opposite by the Youth Hostel.

START: With your back to the road, turn left on a woodland path which parallels the road. It goes through an open area and reaches the junction with the Somerton Road. Just before the junction, turn right down the small lane. This is a No Through Road, Pages Hill, and drops downhill. Continue past a large house and the track becomes a footpath straight on to the Somerset Levels.

1. CROSSING TRACK
Reach a crossing track. Go straight across and over a stile to follow the left hedge in the field to the corner.

Ahead is wooded Dundon Hill and to the right of it, Lollover Hill.

Cross a stile on the left and turn right maintaining direction with the hedge on your right. Go to the corner and cross a stile by a gate. Now follow the left edge and, about two-thirds of the way along, cross left over a stile by a gate. Then turn right and soon join a track, still heading towards the two hills. Continue towards Dundon - the church is up ahead.

2. FARM
Pass a part thatched cottage at Hurst and a farm and carry on to a junction. Go straight over on the lane, starting soon to climb gently. Pass the school sign and then just past the first SLOW on the road, turn right through a wooden picket gate into the lower graveyard. Stay over on the left and

then turn left up the church path, and bend right to the great yew by the church entrance.

3. CHURCH
Just sit awhile and imagine the many centuries and lives that have unfolded since this great yew was planted. The church of St Andrews sits on the site of a prehistoric grove and does have a certain stillness. Inside is a certificate recording the age of the yew as at least 1,700 years.

Leave the churchyard's main entrance and drop left down the drive to the junction with a lane.
If you want to omit the loop to Lollover Hill, turn left on the lane and follow directions from 6. Dundon.
For the main route, turn right on the footpath to Lollover Hill. At a crossing track turn right and then bend left and start to climb towards the hill. Cross a stile by a gate and enter the open access area.

4. TRIG
Make your way up to the trig point at the top to enjoy 360 degree views.

The hill is run by English Nature as a reserve to preserve traditional hillside farming techniques, lynchets, and the wild orchids that grow well here.

Continue on bearing down right to the hedge and corner over a stile . Turn left and in the field follow the right hedge to the corner and continue into the next field. Maintain direction following the right hedge on and left round the first corner.

5. GATE
In the second corner follow the arrow through a gate and now keep the hedge on your left. Just before the next corner, with a farm ahead of you, go left through a wooden gate. Then go straight across the field parallel with the right hedge to a stile on the far side by a gate. Cross and come onto a track.

6. TRACK
Turn left and stay on the track for well over half a mile, passing Lollover Hill and climbing a little. Avoid side turns. Eventually reach a metalled lane on the edge of the village. Go straight on passing the Earth Spirit Centre and reach the village road. Turn left.

7. DUNDON
Stay on the road.and turn right on School Lane. Go to the end, past the school, where a marked gate leads into the field.
Here is the chance of another detour up Dundon Hill to the ancient hill fort.
Detour: For this, go right on the track climbing steadily all the way to the top and then enter the fort, a beautiful area maintained by the Somerset Wildlife Trust.

Gradually more and more butterflies are being recorded here and a good variety of grasses and flora are getting established. The hill used to be quarried and the lias from here was used to build St Andrews Church.

(There is one viewpoint if you go left round the rim and another if you go right and explore the fort across to Dundon Beacon, where you may not only enjoy views but see some of the ravens that are breeding here.)

And then to continue our detour route, return to the open part of the fort where you came in, and go across to the opposite side to find a gate onto a path. Turn right and follow the path along and then bend left and go downhill. It gradually descends in the woodland along the side of the hill to reach the track near the start. Turn right back down to the field gate.

8. FIELD GATE
To continue the main circle: Go through the gate and straight on picking up a slab path which was used for villagers from Compton Dundon to visit the church of St Andrews. Follow it through a number of kissing gates, and over a track by a farm. It leads out to a quiet road.
Turn right on this and reach the main road in Compton Dundon.

9. COMPTON DUNDON
For the pub, cross over and turn right to the village pub, the Castlebrook Inn, open daily, which has a very welcoming atmosphere and a good

garden behind. Return to where you joined the main road.

To continue the main walk, go across the main road to Compton Street.

At the beginning is an obelisk erected by the villagers to commemorate Queen Victoria's Diamond Jubilee.

Turn up Compton Street, following a small stream on the right.

Bend left walking along the back of the village past beautiful old cottages.

Turn right on the lane towards Butleigh and Street.

10. BEHIND TOWN

Bend left on a lane known as Behind Town and start to ascend the hill towards the monument. As the lane bends left, go ahead on the marked stony track (not through the gate) which winds up the hill fairly steadily. Ignore side paths and stiles.

Just before you reach the main road, turn left on a path up into the woodland and follow it for a few minutes to reach an open area and the Hood Monument up on Turn Hill ridge.

11. MONUMENT

This tall column memorial to Admiral Sir Samuel Hood (1762 1814) is sadly, today looking neglected. Built in the c19th, it commemorates the spectacular career of a local boy who left home at 14 to join the Navy and went on to become an Admiral. Originally it was linked to the family home at Butleigh by a mile-long avenue of cedar trees. There are great views to Glastonbury Tor.

Continue on passing the monument on your right, and follow the path into trees. Fork left fairly shortly and

continue on parallel with the road over right. Maintain direction through the woods dropping down to reach a side lane.

Turn right. Ignore a stony sunken track on the left and after a few more yards, go left through a gate into an open area of grassland.

Now just continue on with great views across to where you have just walked - Dundon Hill and Lollover Hill - climbing gently, going through one gate and on and eventually reach a gate into National Trust land on Collard Hill.

12. COLLARD HILL

Here is a beautiful stretch straight on along the ridge (stay up, don't fork down left) and if you are fortunate with the weather,enjoy the sunshine and magnificent views.

This area has become a habitat for the very rare Large Blue Butterfly which about 25 years ago was extinct in this country, but they were reintroduced from Sweden.

Drop downhill following the right fence and reach Marshall 's Elm junction on the main road with the Ashcott Road straight ahead.

Here, on the former elm, it is said, some of the Kings' men hanged rebels after the Monmouth Rebellion.

To ring the changes, go ahead on the Ashcott Road on the righthand side (not on the left as you did at the start) following the path to the Youth Hostel, with the road on your left.

The Castlebrook Inn, Compton Dundon, 01458 443632

Notes